My New Book of Words 1

Nina Gontar

New South Wales

Name: _____

My New Book of Words 1: New South Wales

Text: Nina Gontar
Illustrations: Nina Gontar
Editor: Jarrah Moore
Designer: Karen Mayo
Production controller: Renee Cusmano

Acknowledgements
Dedicated to my son Justin, with thanks for the happy memories and hopes for a successful future.

ISBN 978 0 17 018858 6

Cengage Learning Australia
Level 7, 80 Dorcas Street
South Melbourne, Victoria Australia 3205
Phone: 1300 790 853

Cengage Learning New Zealand
Unit 4B Rosedale Office Park
331 Rosedale Road, Albany, North Shore NZ 0632
Phone: 0800 449 725

For learning solutions, visit **cengage.com.au**

Printed in Australia by Ligare Pty Ltd
3 4 5 6 7 8 9 19 18 17 16 15

Contents

The Alphabet

a b c d e f g h i j k l m n o p q r s t u v w x y z

apple **a**

balloons **b**

cat **c**

dog **d**

egg **e**

fish **f**

girl **g**

horse **h**

igloo **i**

jam **j**

kite **k**

lamb **l**

mushrooms **m**

needle **n**

owl **o**

pig **p**

queen **q**

rabbit **r**

snail **s**

tent **t**

umbrella **u**

vegetables **v**

whale **w**

X-ray **x**

yoyo **y**

zip **z**

A B C D E F G H I J K L M N O P Q R S T U V W X Y Z

4

Rhyming Words

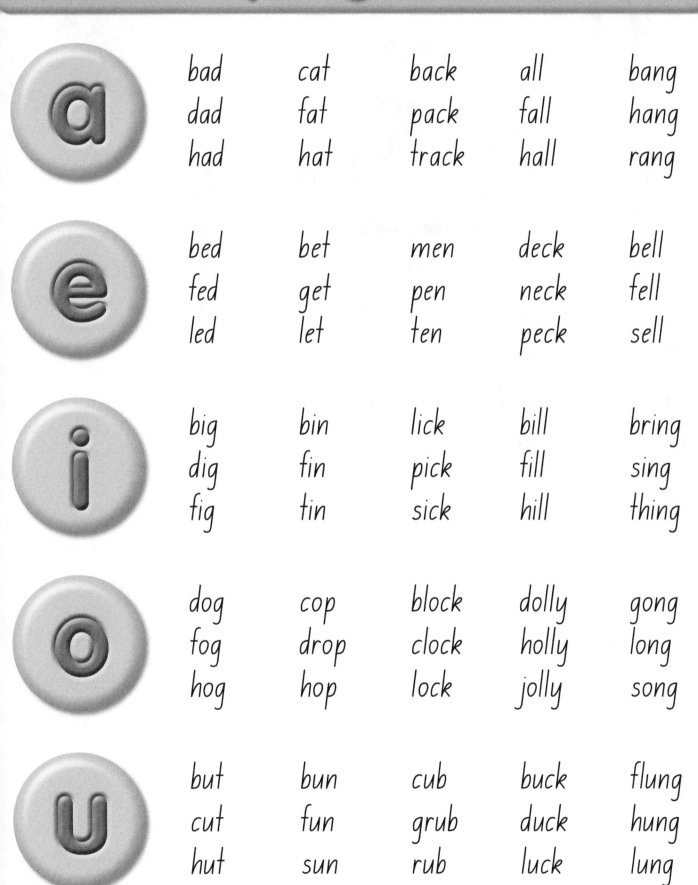

a				
bad	cat	back	all	bang
dad	fat	pack	fall	hang
had	hat	track	hall	rang

e				
bed	bet	men	deck	bell
fed	get	pen	neck	fell
led	let	ten	peck	sell

i				
big	bin	lick	bill	bring
dig	fin	pick	fill	sing
fig	tin	sick	hill	thing

o				
dog	cop	block	dolly	gong
fog	drop	clock	holly	long
hog	hop	lock	jolly	song

u				
but	bun	cub	buck	flung
cut	fun	grub	duck	hung
hut	sun	rub	luck	lung

ants

apple

April
August
Australia

about	all	as
add	am	ask
after	and	at
age	any	aunt

New Words

Rhyming Words for

bad
glad
had
sad

My **dad** gets up early.

_____

_____

_____

_____

bag
gag
sag
tag

These are my **flags**.

_____

_____

_____

back
lack
pack
stack

I have a **black sack**.

_____

_____

_____

bang
gang
hang
rang

I **sang** this song.

_____

_____

_____

"ai" or "ay"?

I can play in the rain.

again	paint
aid	rain
bait	stain
chain	train
main	vain
paid	wait

New Words

_____ _____

_____ _____

_____ _____

_____ _____

_____ _____

_____ _____

away	play
day	ray
gay	say
holiday	stay
lay	today
pay	way

New Words

_____ _____

_____ _____

_____ _____

_____ _____

_____ _____

_____ _____

b

B

butterfly

bees

Ben
Benita
Brisbane

back	before	birthday
bag	behind	book
be	between	boy
because	big	by

New Words

Blends

bl	black blast blind block blue	
br	brag brain bread bring brown	
cl	clam clap class clip clock	
cr	crab crack crash cross cry	
dr	drag draw dress drip drop	
fl	flag flat flip flop fly	
fr	free fresh friend frog from	
gl	glad glass glove glow glue	
gr	grab grand green grin grip	
pl	plan play please plug plus	
pr	press pretty prince print prowl	
sl	slam sleep slid slip slow	
sm	small smart smell smile smoke	
st	stand step sting stop story	

C

cat

cow

Canberra
Christmas
Christopher

cake	car	come
call	clap	could
came	climb	cry
can	colour	cup

_____
_____
_____
_____

New Words

When "c" and "h" stand next to each other ...

ch is their new sound.

champ	check	chips
chance	chest	choke
chat	chill	choose
cheat	chin	chop

chickens

_____

_____

_____

_____

_____

arch	peach
beach	pinch
bench	reach
ditch	rich
fetch	search
French	teach
March	teacher

wat**ch**

Words Ending in "ck"

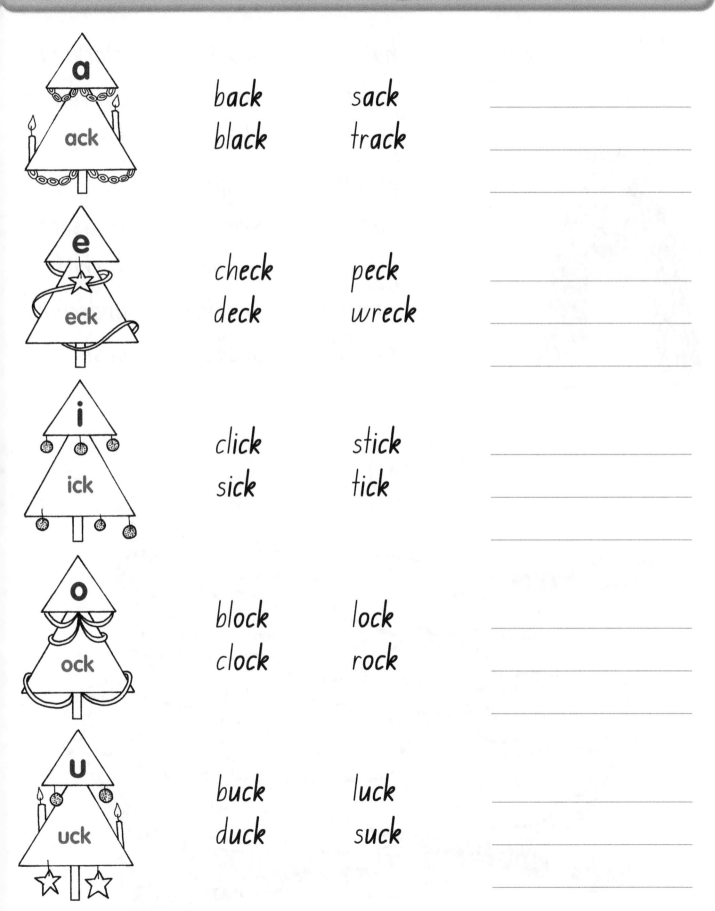

a — ack

back   sack
black   track

_____

_____

_____

e — eck

check   peck
deck   wreck

_____

_____

_____

i — ick

click   stick
sick   tick

_____

_____

_____

o — ock

block   lock
clock   rock

_____

_____

_____

u — uck

buck   luck
duck   suck

_____

_____

_____

Clothes

belt	cap	hat	scarf	stockings
boots	coat	jacket	shirt	swimmers
	dress	jeans	shoes	thongs
	gloves	jumper	singlet	tie
		pants	skirt	trousers
		pyjamas	slippers	T-shirt
		raincoat	sneakers	underwear
		sandals	socks	vest

Colours

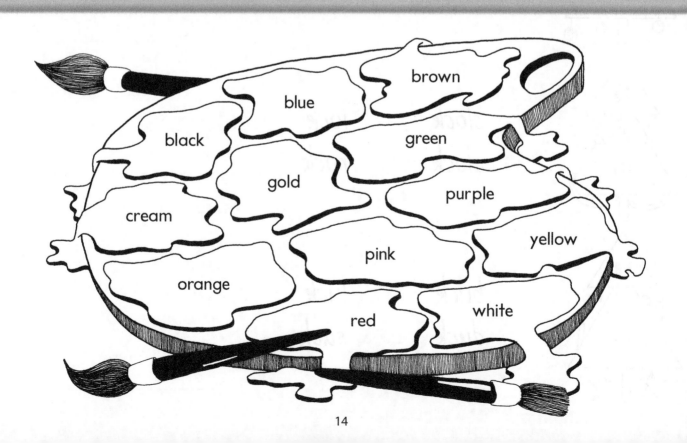

brown
blue
black
green
gold
purple
cream
yellow
pink
orange
red
white

Contractions

Join two words together.

Make one new word called a contraction.

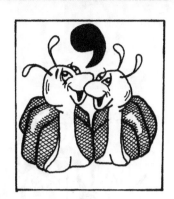

I am an apostrophe!

I am written to show you where the missing letters were.

There I am!

I'm taking the place of the letter **a** in **am**.

I + am = I'm

My list of contractions

are + not = **aren't**

can + not = **can't**

did + not = **didn't**

have + not = **haven't**

I + had = **I'd**

is + not = **isn't**

that + is = **that's**

was + not = **wasn't**

you + are = **you're**

d   dog   **d**inosaur   **D**

Darwin
December
DVD

dance	do	dozen
day	does	draw
dear	dollar	drop
dig	down	dry

New Words

Adding "ed"

bang	help	limp	pick	
banged	helped	limped	picked	
bark	hope	mend	play	
barked	hoped	mended	played	
call	jump	park	thank	
called	jumped	parked	thanked	

Double the last letter before you add the new ending.

bat	hop	rob	tip	
batted	hopped	robbed	tipped	
drop	nod	stop	trip	
dropped	nodded	stopped	tripped	
grab	pop	tap	whip	
grabbed	popped	tapped	whipped	

e / E

echidna

elephant

Easter
Ellen
Eric

each   egg   everybody
ear   elbow   everyone
easy   empty   everywhere
eat   every   eye

_____
_____
_____
_____

New Words

_____ _____ _____
_____ _____ _____
_____ _____ _____
_____ _____ _____
_____ _____ _____
_____ _____ _____
_____ _____ _____

Rhyming Words for

fed
led
red
sled

This is my **bed**.

_____

_____

_____

_____

jet
met
net
pet

This duck is **wet**.

_____

_____

_____

_____

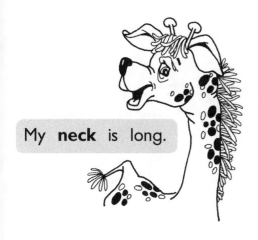

My **neck** is long.

check
deck
peck
wreck

_____

_____

_____

I **fell** over.

bell
shell
tell
well

_____

_____

_____

"ea" or "ee"?

I can see the sea.

beat	leap
cheat	meal
deal	meat
eat	neat
heat	real
heater	seat

New Words

_____ _____

_____ _____

_____ _____

_____ _____

bee	keep
deep	queen
feel	reed
feet	seed
heel	seen
keen	week

New Words

_____ _____

_____ _____

_____ _____

_____ _____

f | **F**

frogs

fish

Fatima
February
Friday

_____
_____
_____
_____

family	few	for
fast	first	friend
father	fly	from
fell	football	funny

New Words

_____ _____ _____

_____ _____ _____

_____ _____ _____

_____ _____ _____

_____ _____ _____

_____ _____ _____

Family Photograph

parents

man
father
dad

woman
mother
mum

relatives

uncle
aunty

children

boy
son
brother
teenager

baby
child
infant

girl
daughter
sister
kid

grandparents

grandmother
grandma
nanna

grandfather
grandpa
poppy

cousins

niece
nephew

grandchildren

grandson
granddaughter

Feelings

I feel
angry.

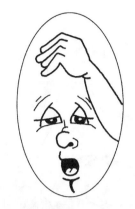

I feel
embarrassed.

I feel
excited.

I feel
happy.

I feel
mean.

I feel
proud.

I feel
scared.

I feel
surprised.

I feel
upset.

Fruit

pineapple

grapes

banana

apricots

watermelon

pear

peach

oranges

lemons

strawberries

apples

cherries

Farm

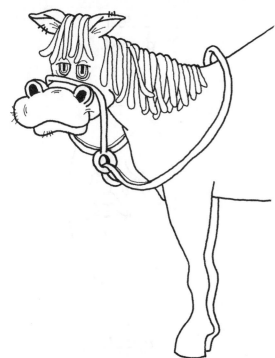

barn	fences	paddock
bull	field	pig
calf	foal	pony
cattle dog	goat	ram
cow	goose	rooster
crops	guinea pig	shed
donkey	harvester	sheep
duck	hen	tractor
duckling	horse	truck
farmer	lamb	water tank

goat

girl

Gavin
Germany
Gina

game	glue	good	_____
gave	go	grab	_____
give	goes	great	_____
glass	gone	grow	_____

New Words

Garden

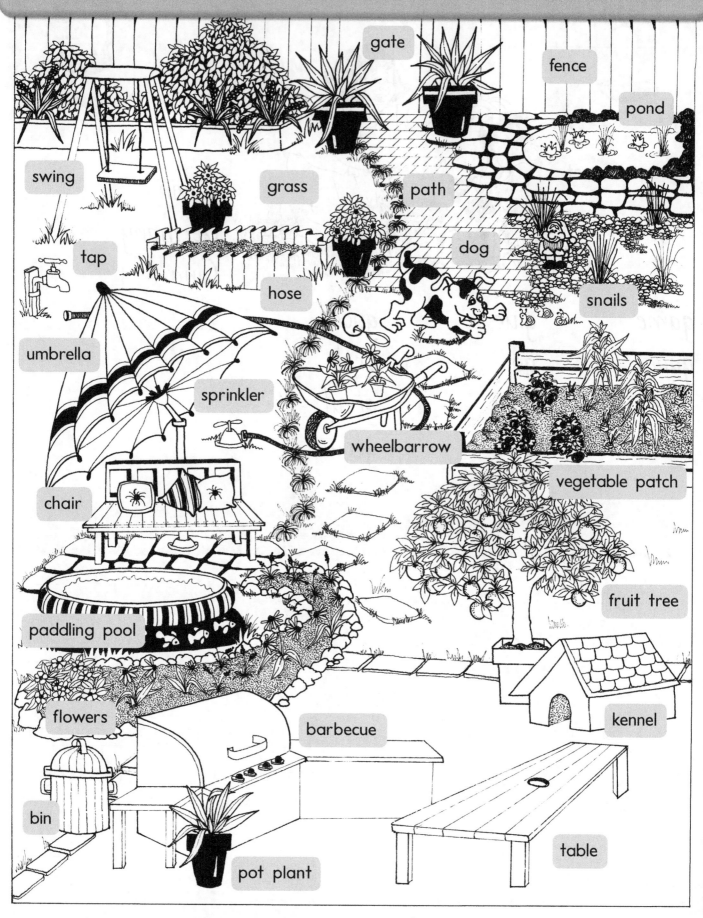

gate

fence

pond

swing

grass

path

dog

tap

hose

snails

umbrella

sprinkler

wheelbarrow

vegetable patch

chair

fruit tree

paddling pool

flowers

barbecue

kennel

bin

table

pot plant

h   H

horse

half

Halloween
Hanukkah
Hobart

had   help   his
has   her   hit
have   here   home
he   him   how

New Words

27

Hobbies

exercise

fishing

football

gardening

gymnastics

horseriding

knitting

music

painting

reading

sailing

skiing

snorkelling

soccer

surfing

swimming

insects

ice-cream

I'll
I'm
I've

idea	inside	it
if	into	itchy
ill	is	it's
in	isn't	itself

New Words

Rhyming Words for

Sit!

bit
fit
hit
lit

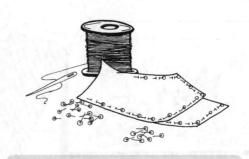

bin
din
fin
win

Pins and needles are **thin**.

_____

_____

_____

_____

_____

_____

I'm **sick!**

flick
kick
lick
pick

I stand **still**.

bill
fill
hill
will

_____

_____

_____

_____

_____

_____

Adding "ing"

The cow needs **milking**.

bark	catch	fish
barking	catching	fishing
help	jump	keep
helping	jumping	keeping

Drop the silent "e" before you add the new ending.

Dancing is fun.

give	hate	love
giving	hating	loving
make	race	take
making	racing	taking

j **J**

jars

juggler

January
July
June

jacket	job	jug
jam	join	jump
jeans	joke	jumper
jet	joy	just

_____

_____

_____

_____

New Words

koala

kangaroo

Kara
Khai
Kokoda Track

Silent "k"

knew

knife

knock

know

keep   kill
kept   kind
key   kiss
kick   kitten

New Words

l L

lion

lemons

Lan
Liz
London

lamb	leg	long
last	like	look
lay	listen	lost
learn	little	love

New Words

Words with "ll"

all

ball	fall	falling	
call	hall	tallest	

ell

bell	tell	telling	
fell	well	yelled	

ill

bill	still	filled	
fill	will	willing	

oll

doll	dolly	hollow	
roll	holly	rolled	

ull

bull	full	bullied	
dull	gull	pulled	

shells

balls

pillows

35

m M

mice

mushrooms

March
May
Monday

made	meet	most
make	mine	mother
many	money	my
me	morning	myself

New Words

mm

comma

common

drummer

hammer

mammal

summer

The baby has a
yummy dummy.

Double the "m" before you add the new ending.

cram	dim	drum	hum
cramming	dimmed	drummed	hummed
ram	slam	swim	trim
ramming	slammed	swimmer	trimming

Me

thumb

eyebrow

eye

ear

wrist

cheek

teeth

mouth

tongue

arm

shoulder

chest

forehead

nose

elbow

waist

hair

chin

neck

hip

fingers

hand

leg

knee

toenail

ankle

foot

toes

heel

feet

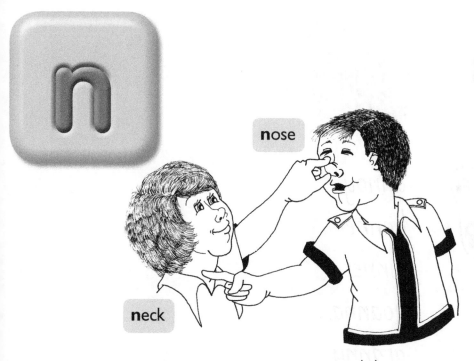

nose

neck

New South Wales
Northern Territory
November

name	never	night
narrow	new	no
near	next	nothing
need	nice	now

New Words

annoy

banner

dinner

goanna

granny

nanny

_____

_____

_____

_____

_____

_____

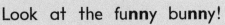

Look at the fu**nn**y bu**nn**y!

Double the "n" before you add the new ending.

fan	grin	pin	plan
fanned	grinned	pinning	planning
stun	sun	thin	win
stunned	sunny	thinner	winning

Words Ending in "ng"

sing

bring
fling
ring
sting

_____
_____
_____
_____

sang

bang
gang
hang
rang

_____
_____
_____
_____

song

gong
long
strong
wrong

_____
_____
_____
_____

sung

flung
hung
lung
rung

_____
_____
_____
_____

Numbers

1	one	first	2	two	second
3	three	third	4	four	fourth
5	five	fifth	6	six	sixth
7	seven	seventh	8	eight	eighth
9	nine	ninth	10	ten	tenth

11	eleven	eleventh	12	twelve	twelfth
13	thirteen	thirteenth	14	fourteen	fourteenth
15	fifteen	fifteenth	16	sixteen	sixteenth
17	seventeen	seventeenth	18	eighteen	eighteenth
19	nineteen	nineteenth	20	twenty	twentieth

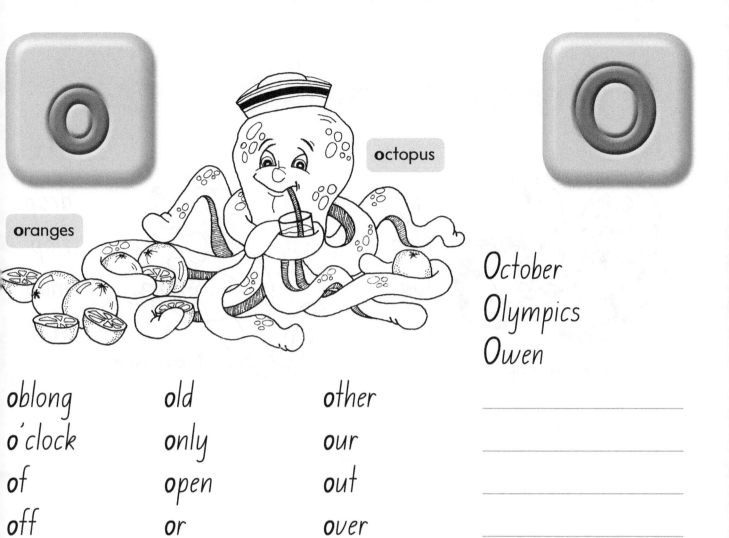

oranges

octopus

October
Olympics
Owen

oblong	old	other
o'clock	only	our
of	open	out
off	or	over

New Words

43

Rhyming Words for

bog
blog
fog
log

I love my **dog**.

_____

_____

_____

drop
flop
mop
stop

I can **hop**.

_____

_____

_____

got
lot
not
pot

Take a ride in a
hot air balloon.

_____

_____

_____

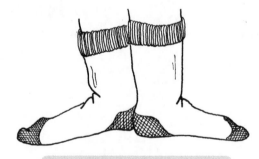

block
clock
flock
rock

My **socks** are warm.

_____

_____

_____

p · P

pelican

parrot

Pacific Ocean
Perth
Phan

paint	pillow	pretty
party	play	pull
pass	please	put
past	pool	pyjamas

New Words

Pepper makes me sneeze!

a-a-a-P-choo..

apple
floppy
happy
nappy
puppy
slippers

Double the "p" before you add the new ending.

chop	clap	drop	hop
chopped	clapped	dropping	hopped
mop	shop	skip	whip
mopping	shopping	skipping	whipped

46

Pets

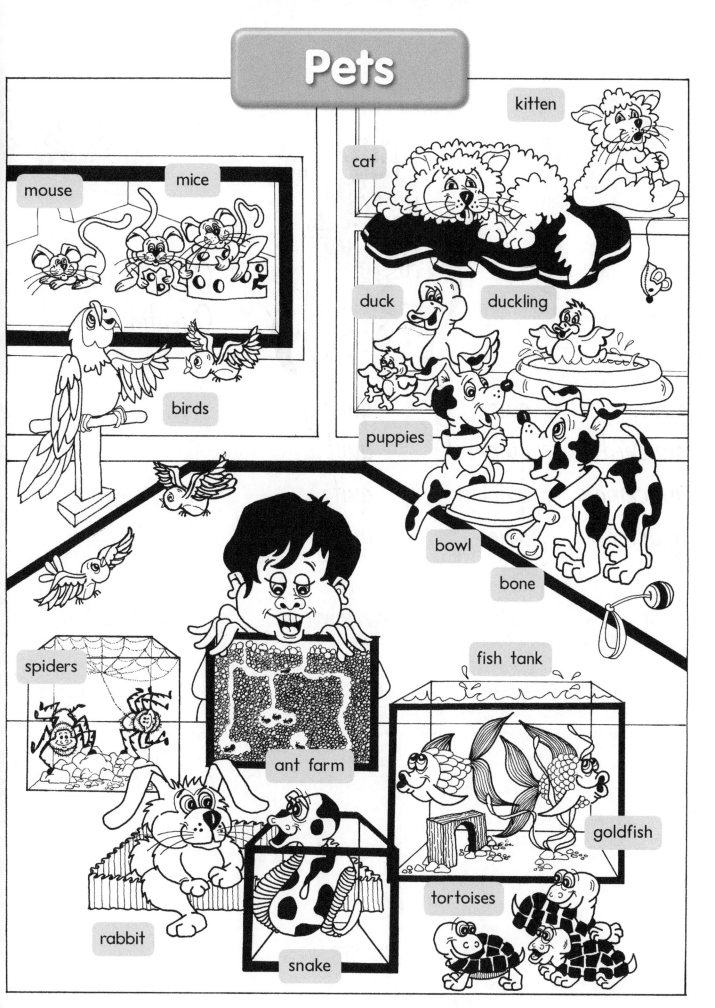

q   Q

question mark

queen

Queensland
Quentin

quack   quick   quietly
quacked   quickest   quilt
quacking   quickly   quit
quarter   quiet   quite

New Words

r · R

rabbit

roses

Raj
Ramadan
Raymond

race	ready	right
rain	recess	room
ran	remember	round
read	ride	ruler

New Words

49

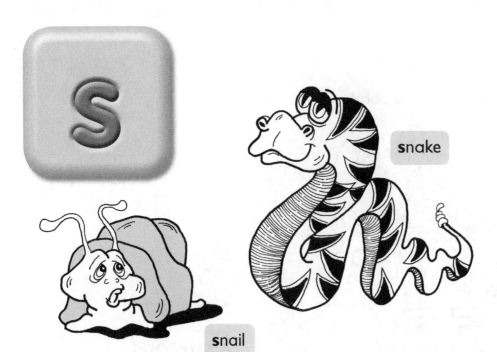

snake

snail

Saturday
September
Sunday

said	sea	sister
saw	see	so
say	she	some
school	sick	someone

_____

_____

_____

_____

New Words

Adding "s"

dog	duck	egg	lick	thing
dogs	ducks	eggs	licks	things

Adding "es"

box	bus	catch	miss	pinch
boxes	buses	catches	misses	pinches

School Classroom

activities
alphabet
art

bookcase
books
brushes

calculator
chairs
charts
computer
craft

desks
drama
draw

drawing-pin
drawings

English
experiments

games
glue

handwriting
history

interactive
  whiteboard

maps
maths

paint
paintings
paper
pencil case
pencil sharpener
pens
printer
puzzles

read
rewards
ruler

science
scissors
stapler
sticky tape

stories
string
sums

table
teacher
television
tests
timetable
toys
trophies

whiteboard
whiteboard
  markers
words
write

School Playground

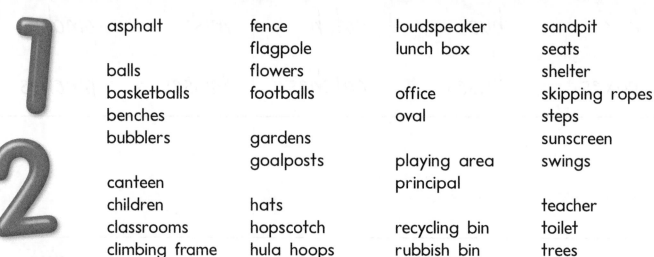

asphalt

balls
basketballs
benches
bubblers

canteen
children
classrooms
climbing frame

fence
flagpole
flowers
footballs

gardens
goalposts

hats
hopscotch
hula hoops

loudspeaker
lunch box

office
oval

playing area
principal

recycling bin
rubbish bin

sandpit
seats
shelter
skipping ropes
steps
sunscreen
swings

teacher
toilet
trees

When "s" and "h" stand next to each other ...

sh is their new sound.

shark

shack	sheep	shock
shade	sheet	shop
she	shin	shot
shed	shine	shut

fish

ash	hush	_____
bash	rash	_____
dash	rush	_____
		_____

Shapes

circle

hexagon

pentagon

square

diamond

oval

rectangle

triangle

t / T

tortoises

tiger

Tasmania
Thursday
Tuesday

take	today	tree
teacher	tomorrow	tried
the	too	truck
to	took	try

_____
_____
_____
_____

New Words

_____ _____ _____

_____ _____ _____

_____ _____ _____

_____ _____ _____

_____ _____ _____

_____ _____ _____

better
butter
flutter
gutter
matter
pretty

I'm little!

Double the "t" before you add the new ending.

bat	chat	cut	let
batted	chatted	cutting	letting
pat	shut	spot	trot
patted	shutting	spotted	trotting

Technology

mobile phone

webcam

screen

joystick

speaker

digital camera

keyboard

mouse

MP3 player

mousepad

game console

blog   joystick
byte   password
chat   photograph
computer   pixel
connect   ringtone
disk   scan
download   search
email   television
game   text
headphones touch screen
icon   virus
Internet   volume

Connect to the Internet.
Delete junk mail.
Download a file.
Exit a program.
Insert a disk.
Listen to music on your
    MP3 player.
Play a computer game.
Scan a picture.
Search the World Wide Web.
Send an email.
Shut down the computer.
Text message a friend.
Upload a photo.

When "t" and "h" stand next to each other ...

th is their new sound.

throw

than	then	_____
that	there	_____
their	these	_____
them	this	_____

thank	thing	_____
thick	think	_____
thief	thrill	_____
thin	thumb	_____

fourth

bother	bath	_____
brother	both	_____
father	broth	_____
feather	cloth	_____
mother	fifth	_____
other	growth	_____
slither	moth	_____

Time

yesterday
today
tomorrow

morning
recess
lunchtime
night

second
minute
hour

spring
summer
autumn
winter

calendar
day
week
weekend
fortnight
month
year

clock
watch
half past
o'clock
quarter past
quarter to

early
before
after
later
soon

Important Dates to Remember

Event   **Date**

My birthday

umbrellas up

Uluru
Umiko
United States

ugly
uncle
under
undo

unhappy
unless
until
upon

upset
us
use
useful

New Words

Rhyming Words for

bug
hug
rug
tug

This is my **mug**.

fun
run
stun
sun

Would you like a hot cross **bun**?

_____

_____

_____

_____

_____

_____

but
cut
nut
shut

I live in a grass **hut**.

buck
luck
suck
tuck

I see a wet **duck**!

_____

_____

_____

_____

_____

_____

V

vase

vegetables

van

vandal

velcro

very

vest

asparagus	lettuce
beans	mushrooms
bok choy	onions
carrots	peas
cauliflower	potato
corn	pumpkin
cucumber	radish
leek	snow peas

Vicky
Victoria
Vietnam

_____

_____

_____

_____

New Words

W

walrus

whale

Wednesday
Wendy
Western Australia

walk	wear	wish
want	went	with
was	were	work
we	will	would

New Words

62

When "w" and "h" stand next to each other ...

**wh** is their new sound.

what
when
which
why

wheels

who
whole
whose

wheel
whip
white
whiz

whale

_____
_____
_____
_____

anywhere
nowhere
whenever
whimper
whistle

whistle

_____
_____
_____
_____
_____

X

box _____

mix _____

ox _____

six _____

X-ray _____

xylophone _____

fox

Y

yacht _____

yard _____

year _____

yell _____

yellow _____

yesterday _____

yoyo

Z

breeze _____

sneeze _____

wheeze _____

zero _____

zip _____

zoo _____

zebra